BECAUSE OF YOU

Breathe

By Jakeel *"SPEAKS"* Harris

About the Author

Jakeel R. Harris is a speaker, workshop presenter and spoken word poet that tackles topics of social justice, leadership, and self-awareness. He promotes equity and equality amongst all community members while focusing his efforts on helping people from diverse and marginalized populations. He encourages everyone to fight against discrimination, racism, and oppression through education, awareness, and civic engagement. He believes that it is essential for people, especially the upcoming generation of leaders, to find their voice, speak their truth and act with purpose.

www.jakeelrharris.com

- Jakeel R. Harris -

TABLE OF CONTENTS

- Jakeel R. Harris -

- Jakeel R. Harris -

- Jakeel R. Harris -

- Jakeel R. Harris -

- Jakeel R. Harris -

Above the Clouds

sometimes I feel like I am a bird

moving rapidly against the wind

fleeting towards an endless sky

where there are no limits

faster and faster

I'm escaping the past of where I used to be

flying towards the clouds of where I want to be

searching for clarity

- Jakeel R. Harris -

Actions vs Words

Actions only speak louder than words when the actions are intentional
and understood
If you don't understand someone's actions
their words can provide clarity

sometimes the proof lies in their dedication
sometimes the truth is buried in their effort
and we are trained to only look at
what's happening on the surface

- Jakeel R. Harris -

Asphyxiate

drown me in your passion
fill my lungs with enough affection
to block the airways to my voice box
suffocate me in your love
until I am silent
I want our love to leave me speechless

- Jakeel R. Harris -

Available

understand that your availability
should only go to those
who make attempts
at putting you first

- Jakeel R. Harris -

Breeze

her existence speaks volumes
but her warmth can encourage
the sun to stop hiding behind the clouds
just to see the competition

she loves so silently, but openly
gives herself to anyone willing to protect the safety of her sunshine

the ocean is jealous of her smile
it wishes it can cause the same flow of emotions that her cheeks produce

she is natural and neglected
a forgotten beauty

- Jakeel R. Harris -

Clarification

you've dealt with trauma, and you're still breathing
you've been heartbroken, and you still love wholeheartedly
you've experienced betrayal, backstabbing, and disloyalty
but still have figured out how to trust
you're constantly under-appreciated and still put your energy into
making others happy
you never let anything stop you from being yourself
and that is something
no one can take from you

- Jakeel R. Harris -

Directions

let the following words below
caress your soul so tight
your spirit
will feel its warmth
continue to let them
touch your mind in ways
that'll make your body climax
from stroking your self-esteem
in the right way
then let these words
rock your doubts to sleep
so you can dream pleasant thoughts of certainty

- you are someone worthy of love and I have no problem giving it to you

- Jakeel R. Harris -

Disappear

disappear into an environment
where connecting to yourself is a
priority
and when you resurface
notice which people took the time to welcome you back to reality

- Jakeel R. Harris -

Ease

when life gets hard
take it easy on yourself
you cannot control the chaos it brings
you can only respond to the madness
and you should never add on to the lunacy
with self-hatred

- Jakeel R. Harris -

Equations

you are not a problem that needs to be solved
you are a formula of unquantifiable greatness that simply wants to be
understood

- Jakeel R. Harris -

Firsts Again (Part 1-3)

the first time she waved at me
my mind just went blank
like canvases
my brain started painting the perfect picture of our future together
but it has always had a hard time envisioning commitment

the first time she approached me
I could taste the nervousness from the bland statements I made when I
tried to speak to her
my words were the perfect ingredients for disaster
and I am way too familiar with that dish

the first time she smiled in what seemed like my direction
my knees lost the ability to function
spiraled out of control
and became crash collision victims
on the road to walking into her life

- Jakeel R. Harris -

SPEAKS

Grocery List of Reminders

here is a quick list of things you are not
    1. worthless
    2. stupid
    3. undeserving
    4. unattractive
    5. basic

let this be a reminder
that your value is priceless
like simple moments of happiness
your intelligence is incomparable
your beauty is perfectly imperfect
filled with gorgeous flaws, a tantalizing figure and a smile that can make
a lifetime of bad days turn into a good moment with just a glimpse
if anyone looks at you from any direction
they'll see the rarity of your essence
and isn't that something worth sharing

- Jakeel R. Harris -

Ignore

ignore the fuck out of people who threaten your joy
people who think it's okay to use your emotions for their convenience
should be removed from your thought process

kick every part of them out of your mental space
and when they try to invite themselves into your physical environment
block every hidden message buried in their intentions

- Jakeel R. Harris -

Invisible

she knew everything about me
including my feelings
and somehow, I still felt unnoticed
it's possible
to get all the attention in the environment
and still experience invisibility

- Jakeel R. Harris -

SPEAKS

Iridocyclitis

sometimes you make it hard to see
the red tints in my eyes
are fiery like the hatred I once had
for a love never felt
you could see the jealousy steaming off of every brain cell in my head
I cover this pain with a Tommy Hilfiger brand hat to feel worthy of
something
so that the sensation left from this envy
prevents me from being blind to the appreciation I have for myself

- Jakeel R. Harris -

Just Keep Swimming

move on
you're too good of a catch
to be stuck in the hands of someone
who will throw you back into the sea
just to see if they can snatch
you out of the comfort of your waters

- Jakeel R. Harris -

Love Afire

we want to be loved so bad
that we set our emotions on fire
thinking someone will be brave enough
to rescue us
but we are surrounded by those who are fascinated with watching
everything around them burn

- Jakeel R. Harris -

L.O.V.E

know that
love could never leave you traumatized
love could never leave you empty
love could never leave you broken
if you've experienced any of that
it wasn't something love did
and that pain you feel is the presence of heartache
don't let this be the reason you call love a mistake

- Jakeel R. Harris -

More Than

she is more than her whiteness
more than her freckles
but be cautious you might find yourself lost in the beauty of the genetic
cluster of skin pigment
she is more than the sisterhood of traveling life lessons she clings onto
she does not place partying on a pedestal or drowns her sentences in
tequila shots
her words are more like mountains of intelligence
landforms created by rising above the surface of doubts
if you stick around long enough you'll see
she is part sophisticated and part experienced
sprinkling humor on every conversation
she is a graceful lily
growing and thriving in the full sight of sunshine

- Jakeel R. Harris -

No, Nah, Nope

learn how to say no
without having the urge
to explain yourself
for a decision
that you made
to ensure your own protection

- Jakeel R. Harris -

Projecting

this message is very important
if you are broken
fragmented pieces from a toxic relationship
you should dedicate your time to healing
instead of projecting your traumas and displaced feelings
onto the next person you end up dating
remember
if you don't give your wounds the proper time it needs to turn into scars
you'll never stop the bleeding

- Jakeel R. Harris -

Self-Caring

if the stability of your mental, physical, and spiritual self isn't a priority
in all of your relationships

especially in the one you have with the person in the mirror

you'll easily fall victim into believing that you should be putting your
energy into satisfying everyone else's needs
except your own

the person who is hurting
hiding
pretending
that the importance of their happiness should be overshadowed
silenced
forgotten

and if anyone tells you
that this is the only way your connectedness stays surviving

reevaluate if your interactions with them
outweigh the long-term effects
of sacrificing your sanity

- Jakeel R. Harris -

Settling

please don't settle for someone
that may be detrimental
for your overall well-being
because you're tired of waiting
for the right person to treat you
like you're special

- Jakeel R. Harris -

Sight-Seeing

when you think the world is blind to your existence

know that I see you for what you really are

the

embodiment

of

ENOUGH

- Jakeel R. Harris -

Sometimes

sometimes you just need to hear how much you mean to someone
other times you need to feel it
I hope my behavior and words gives you that reassurance

- Jakeel R. Harris -

Stopping

stop giving the people who don't deserve you all of you because they
say they love you
they don't love you
they love the way you love them

and if the feeling isn't reciprocal
if they aren't transforming their care for you
into a love worth holding
a love so patient
you won't have to worry
if it'll be there when you wake up in the morning
then stop treating everyone like they deserve you

- Jakeel R. Harris -

Sunsetting

the sunrise sleeps
within her smile
and it hasn't
seen the world
in what seems like
a decade
waiting
for the right person
to set her world in motion

- Jakeel R. Harris -

Swimming Without a Life Jacket

I learned how to swim
by being thrown in your waters
the fear of drowning
from the vast currents of male disappointment
caused me to panic
sinking my ego
to the bottom of your ocean

there I saw
the bones of men
who thought they could sail your seas
on their entitlement
floating by off of pure privilege
believing they could tame your
wild and free nature

but when you underestimate
the depth of a woman's power
you'll get hurricane size tsunami
full of her wrath
strong enough to break masculinity
into fractured pieces

I learned how to swim by appreciating
the essence of your being and
avoided making the same mistakes
as the men
before me

- Jakeel R. Harris -

Taking Care of Myself

I treat myself like I would my son
fix him food
encourage him to eat
explain to him
that missed meals and depression go hand and hand
so fall in love with the taste of satisfaction
until you are full of confidence
watch him brush his teeth
make sure he showers
so that he's so fresh and so clean
he won't have to hide behind the stench of his mistakes
and that he's talking to himself regularly
positively
and when he starts to feel emotional
I let him know
that despite what the world says
it's okay to cry
and honestly
I sit and cry with him
tell him to love
and do it deeply, honestly, faithfully
with anyone he so chooses
he doesn't have to choose anyone
as long as he is loving himself
I make sure I treat him with enough love
that he will hopefully grow up
into someone worth following

- Jakeel R. Harris -

Temples

when you worship this body like a temple
use my skin as your sanctuary
just promise me
I'm the only one you're whispering your prayers to

- Jakeel R. Harris -

SPEAKS

The Key to Her

what do you say to a woman
who has the audacity to be mature
in a time where people her age are still learning how to grow
a woman
whose smile sprints into the room to keep up with her laughter
a woman
strong enough to hold the weight of her doubts in one hand
her pride in the other
balancing beauty standards on her shoulders
and still mustering up the strength to give a planet-size amount of
kindness
to anyone struggling with happiness
to this woman
you say
the world is so much better with you

- Jakeel R. Harris -

To Be Honest

I would give up
half of the time I have left on this Earth
to spend the rest of my life
sharing memories
in a world
where I'm next to you

- Jakeel R. Harris -

Uninvited

if you are constantly living within your head
make sure your thoughts have a safe space to rest
negativity will find a way to barge into your home
and make themselves comfortable

- Jakeel R. Harris -

What I learned from my last relationship

Time is an asshole
like one of those things that knows it's needed and wanted
but chooses to be stingy
it doesn't give a fuck if you're happy
doesn't care if you're spending moments marinating in the sizzling
crockpot that is a loving relationship
it will throw temper tantrums so loud
you will be able to hear it over the sound
of skipping heartbeats
its cries for attention
will become lingering frustrations of "you'll never have enough of me"
repeating a cycle of mistakes
out of your control
until you become nauseous
dizzy
blurred visions make it hard to keep track of them
and if you aren't watching their every move
they will run out on you

- Jakeel R. Harris -

What is Perfect?

lying next to her
basking in the warmth
of our love

- *my definition of perfect*

- Jakeel R. Harris -

YOU

YOU (n.) someone who causes an unexplainable rush of happiness after meeting them for the first time.

synonyms: partner, lover, future, soulmate

- Jakeel R. Harris -

Youth Gone

we ship our experiences
to a place
where we are creating memories.

- Jakeel R. Harris -

Driving Under Instability (DUI)

when you speak out of anger

you're allowing temper

to take control over your emotions

and that kind of recklessness

at the wheel

will drive you towards insanity

- Jakeel R. Harris -

Sprouting

there are too many people
who will try and steal your sunshine

so when you begin to grow
don't announce it
just sprout

and the right people
will appreciate
the flower you become

- Jakeel R. Harris -

Grateful

you are the product
of hopeful sunrises and everlasting tears

your ancestors sacrificed everything
so that you can be granted
the gift of existing

it's the very reason
that makes your ability for growth
capable

in times where your privilege
begins to make your identity unstable
remember all the things they gave up
so you could have the opportunities
they could never dream of

no-one's asking you to be them
but in everything you do
be grateful

- Jakeel R. Harris -

Dreaming Fantasies

In the peace between her sheets
I lay witness to a woman evolving in elegance
while she sleeps
I see my future in the beauty of her soul

with an inability to sleep, I sit and reflect
on how our navigated voyages
of adventurous friendship
put us on the journey to romance
I wonder

If the eagerness in my eyes
will scare her

If the anticipation of her presence
will become too smothering

sometimes I feel like I'm not deserving
then she turns over
and the attendance of my doubts
just vanishes

a fresh ocean breeze of passion passes through my bloodstream
and reminds me
that being next to her is exactly where I need to be

- Jakeel R. Harris -

Staring

I looked into the eyes of depression

letting it know

that I was no longer afraid of its presence

it was in that moment

that I began to find myself again

- Jakeel R. Harris -

Missing out

to that one girl that rejected me
yes, my smile still fires off from the sounds of laughter
my voice still hides at the sight of anyone genuine enough to love me
mistakenly
you passed up on all this greatness
or awkwardness
however you want to put it

I can feel the regret in your text message
you say I miss you
but what you really mean is
I should've taken my chance with you

stop trying to relive the past, it's worthless
my achievements must be burned on the insides of your eyelids
you can't help but see
how well I'm doing for myself
let my glow up shine so bright it blinds you

because if you didn't notice the man
I was transforming to be
you don't deserve to get a glimpse
of the man
I turned into

- Jakeel R. Harris -

SPEAKS

Risk

love loves to leave lacerations lingering loosely on the layers inside your
heart's ventricles
causing catastrophic conflicts creating confusion at the core of your
contemplations
meaning
love is irrational
it has a terrible timing
never understanding
when it isn't wanted or forgiven
love doesn't apologize
knows heartbreak
like it sees it in the mirror

but love
can make fear quiver
insecurities disappear
courage bloom
how love responds to you
depends on if you're willing
to take
your chances with it

- Jakeel R. Harris -

Arrangements

I wonder what love is like

I wonder if I'll learn to love you

I wonder if love really matters

my parents have been together

since their parents decided

and everything seems fine

in fact

I don't remember a time when they weren't happy

I guess

I'll learn to support you

if it makes my parents proud

I'll learn to carry this tradition like my offspring

and protect this idea

that I was made to be given in celebration

I wonder if my curiosity will catch up to my awareness

I wonder if I abandoned this history

will my parents forgive me

I wonder if it's all worth it

- Jakeel R. Harris -

Arachnophobia

I'm terrified of their appearance

the look of the devil reincarnated

bloodsuckers

spinning victims in their web of lies for later consumption

their poisonous venom block signals to the muscles

causing restlessness and intense contractions

some of their bites can go undetected

and kill you before you even come to the realization

that panicking will only cause more fear

this is why I don't trust anything

with more than two legs on it

- Jakeel R. Harris -

Volcanoes

volcanoes remind me that

when your voice is silent

people will dismiss your power

sometimes you'll need to erupt

to avoid self-destruction

and show people

that you're not to be fucked with

- Jakeel R. Harris -

Cutting Loose

her curly hair

lengthy and heavy

similar to the hardships she bares

simply because of her history with neglect

it used to flow majestically

like the moments where the wind and the oceans collide

a representation of what her life was like

beauty in the entanglement

but chaos on the inside

she yearns for attention that feels like acceptance

every piece of her locks tied together in her sadness

only the decision to cut off these burdens

gave her peace

and a brief distraction

from all of life's madness

- Jakeel R. Harris -

Disowned

let rejection

push you into investing

into aspects of your identity

that are constantly disrespected

the neglected parts of your individuality

should become the focal point of the exploration

of your process for self-acceptance

- Jakeel R. Harris -

Translation

love louder than you can speak it

listen attentively

it's not always about what you hear

at times

actions are

the only type of understanding

you'll need to make the right decision

just don't let things

get lost in translation

- Jakeel R. Harris -

Encountered

when I walked into her room I could taste the sweetness from the
passion in the air, it must've been radiating off of the sheets. she moves
towards me, attempting to welcome my companionship with a gesture. a
hug,
something so simple that always felt like vice-grips clinging on to my
every desire. and all I could think about is our bodies intertwining in
slow motion. these instances were like predictions or temptations I
needed to fulfill.

we kiss and I imagine tracing my lips across her skin. hoping to embed
pleasure into places no man has ever been. but I'm patient. I wait for her
to give me the right signal or for the perfect moment to show her body
it can experience outbursts of satisfaction so loud she'll shake in silence.
a climax of sexual excitement goes well with flawless timing.

she guides me to the bed, her sanctuary. where I finally get to enter her
body, the temple. worshipping a figure by giving it an offering. every
piece of me. however, she wants to receive it. every prayer I make is
answered with her moans. sounds that fueled each thrust. I grip her

- Jakeel R. Harris -

waist, pulling her closer and myself deeper, as if I was digging for her soul. despite the length of time my energy is increasing. I start to wonder if she tastes as good as she's looking. I grab her thighs to engulf her elegance. leaving the remnants lingering on my tongue.

We lay in exhaustion. dopamine rushing through our bloodstream and we're connected for a second. so when we looked at each other, we saw the results of pure attraction, raw emotion and an erotic occurrence.

- Jakeel R. Harris -

Raising Men

do you understand
that a father's disapproval could traumatize sons
into believing that masculinity
is determined by the way
his dominance walks into a room
by how much weight his aggression can bench press
by his ability to destroy everything that privileged lies have created

do you understand
that we teach boys to be toxic
I mean masculine
before showing them the manner in which it takes to be authentic

we grow up with a misconception of what respect looks like
we wear fragility like a shitty diaper
that no one wants to change
our fathers instill entitlement
we wouldn't know grateful if it carried us in the womb for 9 months

do you understand
we men
pass down excuses
justifications
as to why sexism runs in our DNA
oppression has been coaching us into being exactly like him
it's time we stop listening
and start rebelling

- Jakeel R. Harris -

Disappointment

don't let the terror of disappointment

be the reason

you make passing up on beneficial

commitments

actions of your everyday behavior

- Jakeel R. Harris -

Complete Me

maybe

the broken parts of you

are the exact pieces needed

to make someone else feel whole

sometimes those same fragments

are faultless

in the mind of another person's

perception

- *to the flawed parts of me*

- Jakeel R. Harris -

Succession

if you want to succeed

your wants and your needs

should be more than just dreams

more than just fabricated components of things that could be

instead

make them your cravings

let them be the alarm that gets you up in the morning

block out the thought that attaining them is impossible

and just focus

because success is not fame, its progress

- Jakeel R. Harris -

Smiling

when my smile gets tired
it falls asleep to sounds of you saying
I will never leave you

it wakes up
every morning
hoping that
it's true

- Jakeel R. Harris -

Progression

learn from your past mistakes
to grow in the complete disarray of the present
maximize the effort you place in being better than you were yesterday

- Jakeel R. Harris -

SPEAKS

Ranting

you're the girl
my emotions talk so highly about

you're the girl
they stumble over their words for

you're the girl
that makes them want to stop being so complex
you motivate their conciseness
their clarity
they've learned to express themselves openly

you're the girl
that gives them
a desire to be alive

according to my emotions
you're the reason for warmness in their bellies
and a breath of inspiration

- Jakeel R. Harris -

SPEAKS

Raining

be like the rain

depositing

fresh water onto

some of the Earths

driest places

a necessity to avoid a travesty

but when the world tries to take advantage

flex your natural properties

become heavy enough

to fall under severe gravity

causing floods

and landslides

reminding people

that a storm is what happens

when there is a disturbance in the atmosphere

teaching people

not to take advantage of your kind nature

or fuck with your environment

- Jakeel R. Harris -

Live or Die

life is too short
for you not to
stand up for yourself

death happens too frequently
for you to take so few chances
at the things you want to accomplish

survival is having the courage
pick yourself up
when the rest of the world
is occupied by limiting risks
because they're so worried about
falling

- Jakeel R. Harris -

Observing

and in the end

we all

are just looking

for love in all the wrong places

seeing it from somebody else's perspective

but never gazing inside ourselves

where it should truly be existing

- *Self-esteem*

- Jakeel R. Harris -

All Falls Down

she was so used to being surrounded by men

who excel at crossing boundaries before respecting them

that she's mastered using silence and rejection as tools to build an

impenetrable barrier

for those who aren't patient enough to wait

as she learns

how to get comfortable

letting the walls of her heart come down

- Jakeel R. Harris -

Self-Care

if I tell you

my selfish behavior is the product of me figuring out how to love

myself

and you respond with anything less than affirmation

I will transform our once trustful relationship

into one

based solely on

avoiding altercation

since you don't seem to add validation to the discovering of my process

you will no longer have the opportunity to observe it

- Jakeel R. Harris -

Insomnia

find someone

you're willing to ruin your sleep schedule for

staying up all night

because the thought of their name

causes you to crave their touch

like a midnight remedy

someone whose name wakes you up in the middle of the night in

excitement

disturbs you with passion

and yearns for your love

like you are their living fantasy

- Jakeel R. Harris -

Becoming an Ally

you must

refuse to perpetuate centuries worth of socialized beliefs

reflect on the differences of your advantageous social treatment

learn that your guilt is freedom

understand you'll never comprehend an oppressed experience

you can only empathize as far as your privilege allows you to

you have to

do more than just feel bad

your silence is still louder than any march or protest

use your voice to echo the reality of the silenced sounds of marginalized

populations

- Jakeel R. Harris -

Growing Up

maturity is less about how much time you need to grow up
and more about how much damage your heart has taken

pain will prepare your future
for the things
your present
was never ready for

- Jakeel R. Harris -

Gossip

be careful when listening to the lies from loose-lipped individuals
claiming they are to be trusted with your innermost secrets

their character
will show you the truth behind all of their intentions

- Jakeel R. Harris -

First Amendment Right

when your experiences sound like muffled echoes down a tunnel of
constant misunderstandings

when your beliefs have gotten comfortable in the reality of their
captivity

your voice will stay in a feedback loop of uncertainty
even though its confidence can move a generation of unknowingly
ignorant

freedom of speech is only given to those whose opinions have always
had the privilege to force themselves to be listened to

understand that oppression and racism have selective hearing

- Jakeel R. Harris -

Facing Bullies

find the fear inside of you
and gain the courage
to whoop its ass
like you were tired of it
taking your lunch money

- Jakeel R. Harris -

SPEAKS

Seasons

just because your seasonal depression has summer days filled with
excitement
doesn't mean you don't need assistance

what do you do on days where the sun
no longer has the energy to help you get up in the morning

when the spring blooms nothing but sadness

when your thoughts find relief in the trauma of your rainy days
and call it normal

eventually you'll have to say fuck your pride and ask for help

- Jakeel R. Harris -

SPEAKS

Shatter

when a man tells you
that you are difficult to love
shatter his ego like you just dropped a glass filled with any memory of
you two ever being together
sweep the broken pieces out of your life

since he has the audacity to run off at the mouth
let's see if he gets tired of chasing after the last remnants of your
relationship

when a man tells you
that you are difficult to love
he is silently and cowardly expressing
that he was never equipped to love you correctly in the first place

- Jakeel R. Harris -

Housekeeping

find someone
who is willing to help you carry your baggage when the handle breaks
does more than watch you struggle as you unpack it

find someone
who isn't afraid
of the sight of your life's dirty laundry
and never judges the chaos it may bring
despite noticing the lingering smell

find someone who enjoys helping you clean, organize, and throw away
the parts of you that needed to be addressed
so you could live in a happy environment

find someone
who is enthusiastic with the maintenance of your love
even if they weren't the ones who caused the damages

find someone
who views your relationship
as a welcome mat
to the home
where your future lives

- Jakeel R. Harris -

To Those Who Need To Hear It

violence doesn't solve any of your problems
but defend yourself
against anyone who wants to start unnecessary problems

don't let anyone tell you that your aggression
is a result of misdirected anger
there's a no emotional guidebook in dealing with danger

if you have to fight your way out of a hazardous situation
become a fucking monster
turn into the hulk
let your muscles expand
destroy everything in your path
until you're the only thing left standing
because at the end of the day
survival doesn't care how you make it

- Jakeel R. Harris -

Woke-ish

you can be "woke" and problematic in the same body

aware and ignorant in the same moment

making disparaging mistakes under idiotic circumstances

being an oppressor, attacker or perpetrator, doesn't come with an IQ

requirement

- Jakeel R. Harris -

Intelligence

knowledge can be defined as the ability to process information

intelligence is how you use it

- Jakeel R. Harris -

Youthful

when you come to grips with your own reality
you'll sometimes lose the peace buried deep inside of you

but when you find the maturity
in the destroyed remains of your innocence
you'll get why
people say
I wish I could be young forever

- Jakeel R. Harris -

Forgiveness

an apology

is a lot like a promise

an expression of reactions towards the behavior or actions of someone

who doesn't want to be abandoned

but forgetting that addressing your feelings should be a priority

disappointment in the form of a lack of consistency

or growth

without change

both are just tools of manipulation

- Jakeel R. Harris -

Reminder for Women

you will always be the motivation for our meaningful actions.

an inspiration for our successes.

the reason for our presence.

your voice can speak purpose into existence.

your touch can heal hearts, just as quickly as it can break them.

your smile can brighten the tunnels of our dark paths.

and when we get lost in the consequences of our innate chaos

we find ourselves looking for the remedy of the pain in the privacy of

your being.

so yes

you have every right to guard yourself against a demographic of entitled

men whose privilege is rooted in your oppression.

you have every right to use your vulnerability as a weapon.

wear the ripped-out hearts of men on your sleeve

to show everyone what happens to those who try to take advantage of

you.

you have every right to sharpen your tongue as you see fit.

- Jakeel R. Harris -

SPEAKS

you must be prepared to stab anyone who thinks their actions don't end
with repercussions.
make them regret doubting your ability to speak up for yourself

if you wanted to stop living the life socialization has planned for you
you have every right to.

if reinvention became the thing you craved in the morning
take two dosages of do whatever the fuck you want.
because you have every right to.

- Jakeel R. Harris -

Head-Start

when life has given you a head start

predetermined your success from the moment of your birth

handed you opportunities as an inheritance

rewarded your ignorance with a newfound sense of entitlement

not being served with preference

makes you believe that you're experiencing serious mistreatment

but when you're so accustomed to privilege

equality will a lot feel like oppression

- Jakeel R. Harris -

SPEAKS

Timing

every success
has had a failure
that came before it

the best things in life
only occur
with perfect timing

- Jakeel R. Harris -

Hits

validation always hits a little different

when you need it

you'll begin to taste that miracle healing called acceptance

soothing your throat

so you never get the urge to regurgitate negative sentences or words

about yourself

and when it sits in the bottom of your stomach

remember not to take those feelings for granted

- Jakeel R. Harris -

Grown

growing up

I learned that

my confidence had the alter ego of skepticism

much like Clark Kent to Superman

except

there were no photo booths to change in

and everyone saw through my disguise

- Jakeel R. Harris -

First generation

our ancestors spent

centuries chasing a better future

from crossing rivers to jumping ships

endured insomnia filled nights of shivering torture

just for a glimpse at opportunity

they learned how to live in the era of dying fantasies

to raise a generation whose first words were freedom

although they weren't alive long enough to hear them

just know all of our successes can be heard from the grave

they live vicariously through us

we are products of their sleepless efforts

and the embodiment of all of their dreams

- Jakeel R. Harris -

SPEAKS

Favorite Song

if there were a song to describe my life

it would probably be called "growth"

I'd listen to it every day

recite the words until I learned all the lyrics

and of course

I'd make mistakes along the way

but eventually

I'll get it

and when I finally understand the meaning

I won't hesitate to share it with you

I just hope you take the time to listen

- Jakeel R. Harris -

SPEAKS

When the storm hits/temporary

I hear your name when it rains

each drop

caressing the asphalt

exploding upon impact

reminding me of the nights we spent together

those instances of bliss only satisfy my desires until the clouds clear

then I remember how our love was so temporary

- Jakeel R. Harris -

Don't break

she learned how to hold herself up
despite the societal judgements keeping her down
criticisms that forced her to create survival
out of catastrophic misery
with every tragedy
she loses a piece of her innocence
and gains the ability to fight for something worth believing in
she worries that she's lost herself in the process

- Jakeel R. Harris -

Miss Fortune

if I had a dollar
for every time I put my heart
into hands that carelessly
shattered promises
like they were playing target practice with my vulnerabilities
I still wouldn't be able to afford
to take my chances with you

- Jakeel R. Harris -

Last Dance

a black man
is forced to *shuck and jive*
their way out of racial stereotypes
learning to *electric slide* their families out of poverty
teaching their daughters to *moonwalk*
because their footsteps are like magic
amazing when seen
but can vanish in a matter of seconds

a black man
instructs his son to *dip*
at the sight of police
and if they are ever held at gunpoint
their hands better *raise the roof*
like they were reaching for another opportunity at living
a black man
must dance to the melody of
barely making it out alive
thank God
rhythm flows through their bloodstream
the beat of survival is pounding on their African ear drums relentlessly

- Jakeel R. Harris -

Wanted

when the amount of interest you have in someone

isn't matched by consistent effort

or communication

you will have people thinking

they aren't wanted

and that kind of confusion

leads to expired emotions

- Jakeel R. Harris -

Attention to Detail

don't let temporary attention
trick you into believing
you need to put effort into someone
you aren't interested in

- Jakeel R. Harris -

Love letter from Cultural Appropriation

to whom it may consume
I hope
this love letter finds you well

after our last encounter
I couldn't help but think about how much your ignorance turned me on
like
the way you came out of that room
wearing "fashion accessories"
that are tied to a culture under colonial rule
was so
attractive

magnificent, how you adopted elements of hip-hop and historical
tradition to become a trend setter
your ability to become a walking forgery is unparalleled
you have transformed cultural admiration into oppressive burdens
damn
you deserve a reward

- Jakeel R. Harris -

SPEAKS

some appreciation

the way you have benefited from your obsessions with what's popular

should be taught to children

I want to teach your strategies to kids

pass down ignorance in the form of innocence will protect them from

scrutiny

tell them

they don't have to be black to tighten their privilege with dreads

a native to wear sacrifice and bloodshed like a baseball team uniform

that sombreros and ponchos are perfect with tequila and racism

I just wanted to take the time to express my feelings and gratitude for

you

Thank you for validating my presence

to whom it may consume

culture and oppression have been having a love affair for ages

so why not bask in its consequences

- Jakeel R. Harris -

Resilience?

life doesn't care whether you're weak
or strong
if you're defenseless
it will try and take advantage of every vulnerability that slow dances
with heartache
every vulnerability
that invites trauma into its bedroom
despite the lack of trust in their decision making

and if openness
has a hard time being intimate with your insecurities
you will crumble at the sight of any challenge
daring you to overcome it

- Jakeel R. Harris -

Tyranny

trauma rules over

a distant land

pushed to the back

of our minds

a place

where there lives people

struggling to find

the right revolution to warrant peace

- Jakeel R. Harris -

Taking Risks

your comfort zone can become a cage

preventing you from realizing the reality of the world beyond its enclosure

blocking endless possibilities becomes the strategy for you to stay in the safety of familiar

but in the rare moment

fear forgets to trap curiosity behind the wall of your bad memories

you'll see

that the world is full of opportunities

the challenge is for you to decide

if you want to step out of those gates

and take the chance at thriving

or continue to protect yourself by not taking risks

- Jakeel R. Harris -

Bane's Memo

darkness can and will consume anyone that gives it the opportunity to
clinch its
malicious warmth onto

so, it doesn't matter if you were born in it
or pushed into its path

if you don't adapt to it
you'll never see the light within yourself

- Jakeel R. Harris -

3 things about being black you only know because you are living while being black

1. What doesn't kill you makes you blacker

Black folk have to joke about the number of times we survived extinction on a daily basis to overcompensate for our fear of being historically targeted. We are told to become comedians of our trauma, creating laughter from the sounds of our ancestor's struggle. I guess the punchline is always funnier when the content is derived from true suffering

2. The way you exist is intimidating

You'll be envied for the culture you have created as a result of oppression and hated for the audacity to be proud of your melanin. This will become the angering spark that ignites the hatred of your presence. Fear will be the epitome of your existence in the eyes of whiteness.

3. Black Women are fucking magic

They are gifted with the ability to cast rhythmic spells from the snap of their fingertips
They can start and stop revolutions with an eye roll, stare, threats of
"I wish you would" and still find the heart to balance the worlds troubles on the laid edges of their curls
Black women can make support appear out of nowhere
pull affection out of top hats
turn water into gratefulness
and for their final act
can transform a broken home into a functioning family
Black women have it so much harder than the rest of us
and still make it look easy

- Jakeel R. Harris -

Manipulation

don't mistake his consistency
for nothing more than a step towards
determining if he wants to be committed

men find ways to disguise manipulation
into passion
and call it love

if he wants to be with you for more than just the amount of time it takes
for you to welcome him into the space where your sexual urges are
freed

he won't have to try to convince you he's striving for commitment
because he already will be

- Jakeel R. Harris -

107

Living For Love

I reached for the last ounce of love you poured me

hoping it still tasted as sweet as the first drop of intimacy in our
relationship

sip by sip

I consumed every bit of it

thinking it will be the nourishment I need to muster up the energy
to keep our love alive

- Jakeel R. Harris -

The Beauty of Being You

despite the pressure of living up to someone else's expectations

there you go being yourself

standing out

in a world full of displacement

- Jakeel R. Harris -

Careful

be careful with how you say *I love you*
the emotions in your voice
can give off the wrong message if the delivery is weak
causing a frequency of uncertainty
and that will sound a lot like
I'm only saying the things you want to hear

- Jakeel R. Harris -

Deserving

never let anybody
try to convince you
that you deserve
anything less than
to be loved effortlessly
wholeheartedly
and full of longing

- Jakeel R. Harris -

SPEAKS

For Colored Boys

embrace your melanin
let it give you enough strength
to break the shackles of a captured soul
lost in the deepening sinkhole that is
oppression

lift your self-esteem
high enough
to liberate your pride in a people whose culture can transform a nation
your continued practice of learning how to live with burdens
will combust into the fragments of motivation
needed to survive in this world

every breath you take
is a rebellious action
every step
a revolution
imagine the mark you'll leave
once you find your voice

- Jakeel R. Harris -

Regrets

my biggest fear
is that
on my death bed
I'll realize
that I should've
treated you better

- *To my heart*

- Jakeel R. Harris -

For Colored Girls

the goddess in you
glistens like the African sun
bouncing off your melanin
it's as beautiful
as witnessing
the ocean reflect
off the moonlight

life-changing
and being around you
is just as
breathtaking

- Jakeel R. Harris -

This is America

to be a man and black in America

is to have your life placed on a pedestal

just so it can be knocked down

stepped on

attacked

and told

it is meaningless

while the whole world

sits in their discomfort

watching silently

doing nothing

- *privilege vs. oppression*

- Jakeel R. Harris -

The Power of Black Girl Magic

she has a womb decorated with tradition
on the walls
nested in the safety of her ovaries lies royalty

but she is cursed to birth
black boys
in a society
that strives to see the joy
being sucked out of them
and for this reason
she puts together divine witchery

avoiding having to parent
a son from an obituary
so her spells don't have to sound like eulogies
she casts love and protection over their bodies

she'll raise hell
just to ensure her heavenly babies
stay breathing miracles

the power of her magic, comes from her melanin

- Jakeel R. Harris -

Love Yourself

when you love yourself
the people around you will feel it too
because love is contagious

so *(pause)*
give yourself so much acceptance
it makes you sick
let the high fever of your self-affirming illness overwhelm you until
it's disgusting
then go out in the world
and infect people

- Jakeel R. Harris -

Born Abused

I am the product of generational poverty and toxic masculinity
the intersectional creation
that I am the result of
is what happens
when oppression and socialization
raises privilege in a basement

feeding it deception and entitlement
as a form of nourishment

barely keeping it alive
under the dire
living conditions
of being a black man

- Jakeel R. Harris -

When They See Us

they become blind to our struggle
while watching our pain manifest

they try to ignore the trauma they caused
with apologies and guilt
as if their tears drowned out the sounds of our screams
our cries of agony

they ask for our forgiveness
without acknowledging the blood they have spilled

when they see us
they're only looking to avoid
our anger

- Jakeel R. Harris -

Still Hoping For Us To Be Together

when my heart tries to perform to a song that isn't your voice
it sings your name in place of the forgotten lyrics
stumbles over the present moment
when trying to dance to the melody
saves a seat for your love in the audience
hoping to see your face in every opportunity to love again

it realizes
you're not there anymore
but continues anyways
giving the concert of a lifetime
because as they say
the show must go on
no matter who's watching

- Jakeel R. Harris -

Questions

when the heartache stops
ask yourself
am I actually healing
or have I just gotten used
to the pain

- Jakeel R. Harris -

Collide

crash into me
break open
the doors to my heart
and call me your
greatest accident

- Jakeel R. Harris -

Monsters

we are taught to be afraid of the monsters under our beds
but we forget how terrifying the demons in our minds are
maybe we are teaching children
the wrong lessons

- Jakeel R. Harris -

Defying Masculinity

appreciate her strength
instead of challenging her power

her impact
shouldn't make you feel weak

- *from femininity*

- Jakeel R. Harris -

In Love

when you're in love
you'll crave to have conversations
about nothing
with someone
who means everything to you

silence will no longer feel like quietness
time will become a living concept of irrelevancy
and you will be perfectly content
in the peacefulness
of a lover's tranquility

- Jakeel R. Harris -

Foolish

and just like that

there I was

willing to risk it all

just to be close to you again

- Jakeel R. Harris -

SPEAKS

4TH OF JULY in 2019

we celebrated our independence
with fireworks loud enough
to wake up families
trapped in concentration camps
disguised as border detention centers

the red, white and blue hues
lit up the night sky
showing an expression of freedom
captivating our attention
no wonder
why we were so blind
to their living conditions

we sang
our national anthem
to the baseline of weeping migrant children
and isn't
that just American
isn't that just the most patriotic thing
you ever heard

- Jakeel R. Harris -

Never Hidden

anyone asking you to hide your true self

out of fear of humiliation

only wants you in their life

so you can be their trophy

views you as some plaque they can be awarded

for dedicating their time

into the possibility

of you becoming

an important piece of their reality

you should never be embarrassed

for being exactly

who you want to be

- Jakeel R. Harris -

Dear Heart

I hope someday
you'll forgive me
for leaving you
with people
who had no idea
how to treat you

- Jakeel R. Harris -

Reality

I miss the lies you told
I miss the way you pretended
to love me
I miss the bored look in your eyes
I miss the heartache
because even though
there were problems when we were together
at least
I still had you

- *missing your presence*

- Jakeel R. Harris -

First Time

I'll never forget
the first time I saw you
it was the day I realized
that a smile
could cause my pride
to crumble
that a laugh
could make my ears
shiver in chills

I remember
how my hands
felt like earthquakes of anxiety
I couldn't contain my excitement
if I wanted to

I'll never forget
the first time I saw you
because
it was the day I realized
that love
had finally made
its introduction

- Jakeel R. Harris -

Leap of Faith

jump into opportunity

imagine landing

feet first onto success

and continue to leave

your footprints

with every step you take

- Jakeel R. Harris -

Evaluation Apprehension

when we live for the satisfaction of others
we become
so concerned
over what they think about us

we place our identity
in the hands of these judgements
hoping the idea of us
makes sense through the eyes someone else

the anxiety that overtakes our actions
can enhance
or impair our happiness
and you should never
give someone that power

- Jakeel R. Harris -

Effort

stop comparing the amount of time, energy and effort
you can put into your relationships
to that of the people receiving it
without first understanding
what their capacity for giving it is

sometimes people aren't capable of being reciprocal
and you have to decide
if the inconsistencies
are worth it

- Jakeel R. Harris -

Life After Death

if I die

because some cop mistook

my breathing for a threat

know that

whatever they say about me

true or false

doesn't justify my death

if the news wants to cover my story

don't show an ounce of empathy

for the people

who are getting away with murdering families

forgive them on your own terms

and at my funeral

don't cry

don't be sad

just revolt loud enough that I can hear it from the grave

make sure that even though I'm dead

you'll keep my name alive

- Jakeel R. Harris -

SPEAKS

Unapologetically Black

it is not your fault
that people are offended
by the act of you
expressing your blackness
matter of fact
be so black
that your clapbacks
sound like chains breaking
let your hair be so natural
that you can grow confidence from its roots
but if you choose to get a weave, sew in tracks, or even extensions
wear that shit so proudly
you could see the black power fist engraved in your edges
or the flow of black excellence in your waves
be so black
that your name
sparks a discussion
no matter how many times people mess up the pronunciation
it's still synonymous with revolution
so if they think
you are being offensive
be blacker
be you
be expressive

- Jakeel R. Harris -

Safety Matters

you do not have to sugar-coat your refusal

because he'll take offense to rejection

no need to transform your language

into something more hesitant

to salvage his feelings

if he doesn't understand your dislikes

it isn't your responsibility to inform him

you do not have to be nice

when you're prioritizing your safety

- Be a bitch. Your safety is more important than being nice.

- Jakeel R. Harris -

Melanin

I know this

my melanin is more than a target

it avoids becoming prey for white hatred

while societal beauty standards neglect its perfection

attempting to erase the soul within the body but still

my melanin is an exotic masterpiece that hyper-sexualized thoughts

try to claim

as if

they could hold onto the idea of objectification

but never embracing the skin

my melanin

is African traditions being embedded in a mixture of complexion

survival engrained in pigmentation

if you study my skins cells

you'll see that my melanin is a genetic superpower

that I will no longer take for granted

- Jakeel R. Harris -

Begging

don't go begging for attention
in places
where you are avoided
and unnoticed

you don't need to gain placement in areas
where people don't deserve you

- Jakeel R. Harris -

The Tribal Soldier: The Real American

he falls from a family tree full of fathers who hated their liver
bloodline made up of traditions and rituals
rites of passage
filled with sacred stories
revealing the history of majestic warriors who walked a generation
towards survival
but oppression runs deep in his DNA
poverty rooted in the soil of stolen land he had his first kiss on
landmarks that were once home to cultural celebrations
colonizers showed up like imposters
tricking themselves into believing that stealing property was natural
normalizing marauding
until white guilt prompted them into
giving back selected pieces of looted land so he could have a space to
practice his broken English on
every syllable sounding like acculturation
enlisted in an army whose past consisted of thieves who pillaged tribal
homelands
and he still says he'd die for this country
ironically his ancestors did too
and society has the nerve to say he lacks pride
when his people invented patriotism

- Jakeel R. Harris -

Neha's Language

her speech
is derived from kindness
it's a particular dialect of niceness
when translated to "American"
most people don't understand it
or are ignorant to the subtle inflections in the soft tone
so she tries to transform this linguistic masterpiece
into a common language
but somehow
the conversion is a little wonky
if you listen closely
you will notice
the culture wrapped around her tongue
you can hear the tradition in her voice
sounds that speak freedom into the soul
and more people
need to learn
how to embrace it

- Jakeel R. Harris -

SPEAKS

Taryn's Story

once upon a time
there was a girl who gave
all of her love
to loved ones
so they never were the ones to ever feel
what it's like to have none of it

this girl
broke her back to fix smiles
damaged by unwarranted struggle
sprained her wrist cooking her sibling's multiple servings of happiness
seasoned with forgiveness
for good measure
just in case there were days where she didn't get the ingredients right

this girl
carries love in her wallet
hoping to cash in on its benefits
and isn't afraid to give it away
to someone else in need of it

once upon a time
there was a girl who gave
all of her love
to loved ones
I hope she includes herself in the process

- Jakeel R. Harris -

Losing Love

I can admit that love scares me
there's something about being embraced with intimacy that's just too
new to me

I like my routine
pushing people away when they seem to get close enough to alter my
emotions

I can admit
that I have driven away more people than I wanted to
used isolation as an excuse for disconnecting with those bringing me
more love than I deserve

I can admit
that I have been a faulty door
appearing to be open but closed until further notice
I'm broken but functional
and done waiting to be fixed

I can admit
I've been letting my relationships slip through my fingertips
losing sight of how perfect I have it

- Jakeel R. Harris -

Unfair

it's unfair
that a man
will desire a woman with their full heart
but love them half-heartedly

wonder why their relationship is dying
when the reason for its stunted growth lies in the deficiency of the
enthusiasm he once had for a woman all deserving
the absence of effort is the cause of the breakdown in commitment
confusion in the words that once sounded like faithfulness

stability has become a lingering question
in her mind
the lack of consistent attention buries the belief of a future together
the toxic presence of his selfishness at her expense ends their intimate
interactions
but she blames herself for not trying hard enough to salvage the
damaged wreckage she calls her soulmate

it's unfair
that men
use 'masculinity', the destruction of everything sensitive, as an excuse
to attempt to ruin a beautiful angel's process in becoming a goddess

- Jakeel R. Harris -

Shadow Talk

sorry I don't speak to you enough
sorry I hold my tongue in your presence
sorry I hide during your darkest times
but remember
the light the shines in you
is the reason I exist
sorry I forget
I forget how affirmation
can turn motivation
into the perfect performance
to overcome the dangers of loneliness
sorry I don't express myself as much as I need to
but if you ever find yourself worrying
know this
to me
you have always been
someone worth following

   - *message from your shadow*

- Jakeel R. Harris -

SPEAKS

Growing up to be the Sun

eventually

you will shine so bright

that the moon will ask you for advice

and when that day comes

explain to it

that you rose from the darkness

by becoming a star

- *to the sun*

- Jakeel R. Harris -

146

Note from the Author

Thank you for reading!

Self-growth begins with open-mindedness and belief in one's abilities. Growth is the life-long process that isn't an individual journey, but one that starts with self-realization. A willingness to learn and having genuine empathy are essential steps in determining how to treat people fairly and justly. Strong relationships are kept stable with honesty and building trust. Sustainable development is the pathway to social justice, economic growth, and self-perseverance.

*For everyone who helped inspire these poems, this book is **BECAUSE OF YOU.***

- Jakeel R. Harris -